A Gift For:

Amber Lynn

From:

Grandpa & JoAnn

"_Happy Reading !_"

Published by Hallmark Gift Books,
a division of Hallmark Cards, Inc.,
Kansas City, MO 64141
Visit us on the Web at Hallmark.com.

Editorial Director: Carrie Bolin
Editor: Kim Schworm Acosta
Art Director: Chris Opheim
Designer and Production Designer: Bryan Ring

ISBN: 978-1-59530-700-2
LPR1401

Printed and bound in China
JUL14

There's Snowbody Like You!

By Barbara Loots

Illustrated by Mike Esberg

Chillbert was little as snowchildren go.

He'd been waiting and waiting for his turn to grow.

His dad said, "Don't worry. In no time, you'll be

the star of the team! Just be patient. You'll see!"

Out at the Ice Park, the Whoop-De-Do Slide
had a sign that said: YOU MUST BE THIS TALL TO RIDE!
Chillbert was sad, but he tried to be brave
as he watched all his friends zoom away with a wave.

Heading home he thought, "There's some work I can do!
I'll offer to help on the light-stringing crew!"

He stepped up with Crystal and Drifty and Bob—
but somebody bigger got picked for the job.

When Chillbert got home, he was not feeling good.

He thought, "There's a lot I *would* do if I could!"

His dad said, "You sure could be helpful to me—

let's go to the farm and pick out a nice tree!"

Some Flurryville kids were excited and glad
to hop in the sleigh with their friend and his dad.

They laughed as they left for a time filled with fun—
a colorful crowd in the bright winter sun.

At Perfect Pine farm, they fanned out to explore
some fields and thick woods they had not seen before.

Blizzy discovered a pond that looked nice
and decided to go for a slide on the ice.

CRAAAAACK!!! went the ice. What a terrible break!
The part Blizzy stood on split loose in the lake!

Everyone came when they heard Blizzy shout.

"Help me!" he cried as the ice drifted out.

Chillbert spoke up. "Listen! I have a plan!
I'm willing to try it—I think that I can.
I'm short and I'm light; if you hang on to me,
I'll wiggle right out on the branch of that tree!"

So Chillbert climbed up and inched out on the limb,
while his friends joined together and held on to him.
He threw out the rope that he had in his hand
and with one mighty pull tugged their friend to the land.

Everyone cheered, "Chillbert's one gutsy kid!
There's snowbody else who could do what he did!"
His dad was all smiles. "You're the best there could be,
and I'm proud of you, Son. Now, let's pick out our tree!"

Chillbert was thrilled when the chance came along
to show he was kind and courageous and strong.
Even somebody small can be useful and smart,
and you're never too little to have a big heart.

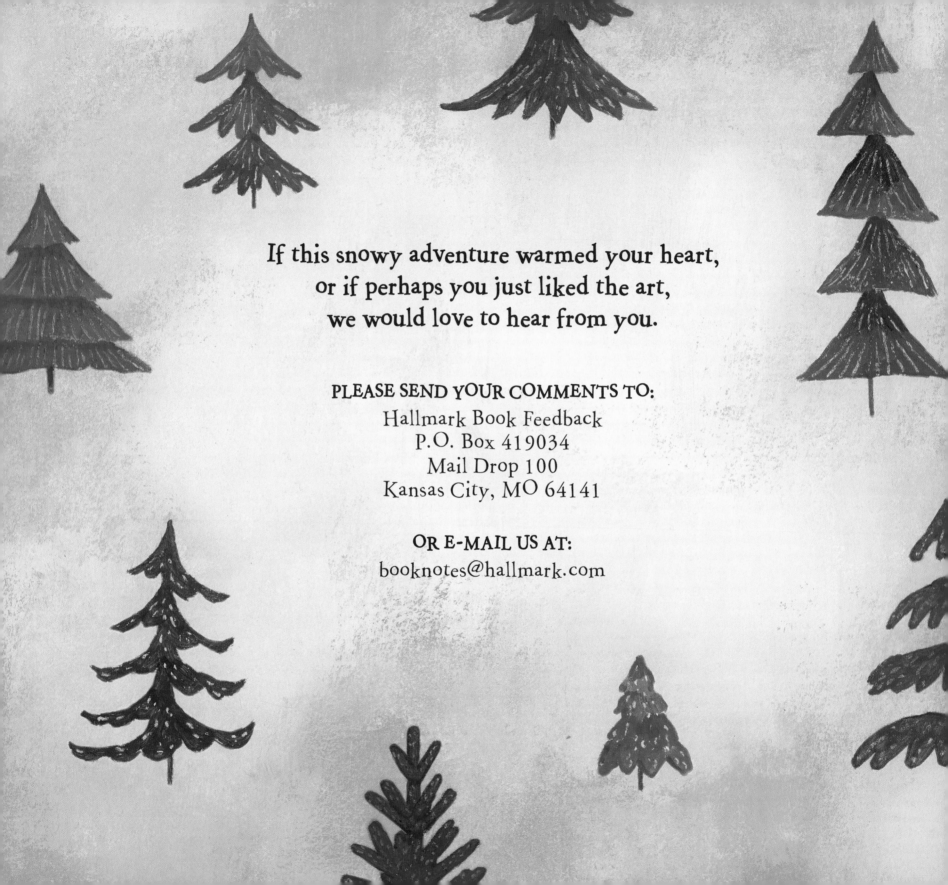

If this snowy adventure warmed your heart,
or if perhaps you just liked the art,
we would love to hear from you.

PLEASE SEND YOUR COMMENTS TO:
Hallmark Book Feedback
P.O. Box 419034
Mail Drop 100
Kansas City, MO 64141

OR E-MAIL US AT:
booknotes@hallmark.com